P9-EEI-755

HERBIVORES

by Dougal Dixon

Gareth Stevens Publishing
A WORLD ALMANAC EDUCATION GROUP COMPANY

CONTENTS

Please visit our web site at:
www.garethstevens.com
For a free color catalog describing Gareth
Stevens' list of high-quality books and
multimedia programs, call 1-800-542-2595
(USA) or 1-800-461-9120 (Canada). Gareth
Stevens Publishing's Fax: (414) 332-3567.

Library of Congress Cataloging-in-Publication Data
available upon request from publisher. Fax (414) 336-0157
for the attention of the Publishing Records Department.

ISBN 0-8368-2916-6

This edition first published in 2001 by
Gareth Stevens Publishing
A World Almanac Education Group Company
330 West Olive Street, Suite 100
Milwaukee, WI 53212 USA

This U.S. edition © 2001 by Gareth Stevens, Inc.
First published by ticktock Publishing Ltd., Century
Place, Lamberts Road, Tunbridge Wells, Kent TN2
3EH, U.K. Original edition © 2001 by ticktock
Publishing Ltd. Additional end matter © 2001 by
Gareth Stevens, Inc.

Illustrations: John Alston, Lisa Alderson,
Simon Mendez, Luis Rey
Gareth Stevens editor: David K. Wright
Cover design: Katherine A. Kroll
Consultant: Paul Mayer, Geology Collections
Manager, Milwaukee Public Museum

Printed in Hong Kong

1 2 3 4 5 6 7 8 9 05 04 03 02 01

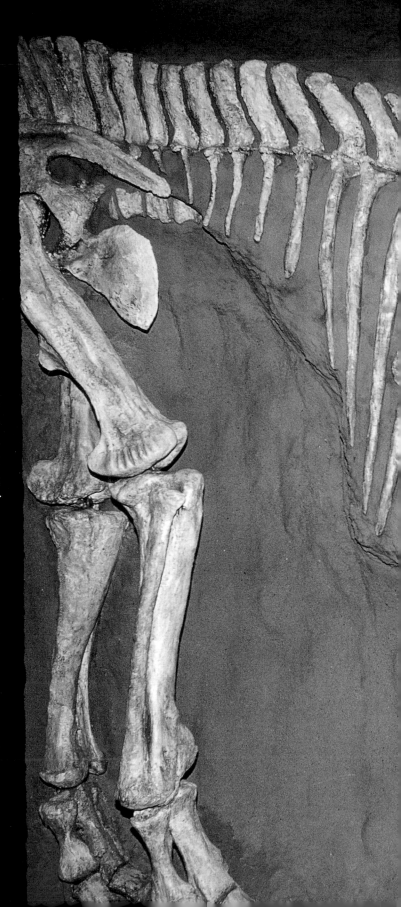

HERBIVORES

MUSSAURUS

The smallest dinosaur skeleton known belongs to a prosauropod. This *Mussaurus* is small enough to be held in the the palm of a human hand. We know it is the skeleton of a baby or an embryo, however, because the eyes and feet are bigger in relation to its body size than they would be in an adult, and its bones are not totally fused together. An adult *Mussaurus* would have been about 10 feet (3 meters) long.

SKULL COMPARISON BETWEEN A HERBIVORE AND CARNIVORE

PLATEOSAURUS

- *Jaw articulates below level of teeth.*
- *Leaf-shaped teeth with continuous cutting edge.*
- *Coarsely serrated teeth for shredding leaves and shoots.*
- *Teeth more or less the same size.*
- *No gaps between teeth.*

TYRANNOSAURUS

- *Jaw articulates at point level with teeth.*
- *Strong, spike-shaped, piercing teeth used for gripping and killing.*
- *Finely serrated saw-edged teeth like a steak knife.*
- *Teeth often break off and new ones grow in their place, creating a snaggle-toothed appearance.*
- *Teeth have gaps between them.*

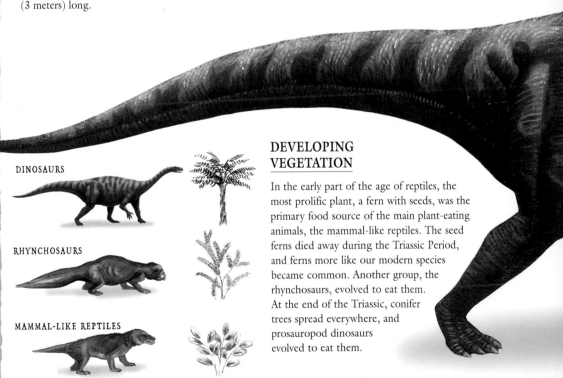

DINOSAURS

RHYNCHOSAURS

MAMMAL-LIKE REPTILES

DEVELOPING VEGETATION

In the early part of the age of reptiles, the most prolific plant, a fern with seeds, was the primary food source of the main plant-eating animals, the mammal-like reptiles. The seed ferns died away during the Triassic Period, and ferns more like our modern species became common. Another group, the rhynchosaurs, evolved to eat them. At the end of the Triassic, conifer trees spread everywhere, and prosauropod dinosaurs evolved to eat them.

THE FIRST PLANT-EATING DINOSAURS

Plant-eating dinosaurs (herbivores) were the real giants of the Mesozoic Era. Among their ranks were the mighty *Diplodocus* and *Seisomosaurus*, the largest animals ever to walk our planet. Herbivorous reptiles are known from the early part of the Carboniferous Period, 350 million years ago. The first herbivorous dinosaurs evolved in the Late Triassic Period, appearing about the same time as carnivores. Because both groups of dinosaurs have similarly formed hipbones, we know that the plant eaters are closely related to meat-eating dinosaurs.

PANGAEA

The world was very different in Late Triassic/Early Jurassic times. All the continental landmasses were together in one area, called Pangaea. This meant that animals of the same kind could migrate everywhere and is why we find the remains of almost identical animals all over the world, from Australia to North America.

PLATEOSAURUS

The first plant-eating dinosaurs belonged to the prosauropod group. *Plateosaurus* was a typical prosauropod. It had a long neck and small head, but perhaps its most important feature was its big body. To process plant matter, a herbivore needs a far greater digestive system than a carnivore. The prosauropod's heavy mass of intestines, carried well forward of the hips, would have made the animal too unbalanced to spend much time on its hind legs, so prosauropods became four-footers early in their history.

TRIASSIC 248-206 MYA	EARLY/MID JURASSIC 206-159 MYA	LATE JURASSIC 159-144 MYA	EARLY CRETACEOUS 144-99 MYA	LATE CRETACEOUS 99-65 MYA

HELPLESS PREY

Paleontologists have found the remains of a prosauropod *Euskelosaurus* in Upper Triassic rocks in South Africa and Switzerland. The bones of its feet and legs are preserved, but the rest of the skeleton is broken up and scattered. Teeth of crocodile-like reptiles and carnivorous dinosaurs are among them. From this we suppose that *Euskelosaurus* became stuck in mud and, while struggling helplessly, was attacked by meat eaters.

RIOJASAURUS

THECODONTOSAURUS

ANCHISAURUS

LIFE OF THE PROSAUROPODS

Ever since plants have existed, plant-eating animals have fed on them, and ever since plant-eating animals have existed, meat eaters have, in turn, fed on them. This type of food chain can still be seen on the grasslands of Africa, where herds of herbivorous wildebeest and zebra graze on low vegetation and are preyed on by prowling carnivores such as lions and cheetahs. It was no different with dinosaurs. Prosauropods fed on the trees and were themselves stalked by meat eaters.

TRACKWAYS

The footprints called *Navajopus* from Lower Jurassic rocks of Arizona perfectly match the foot bones of a typical prosauropod, with big hind feet and smaller front feet, each with four toes and inwardly curved claws. They are likely to have been made by a small *Thecodontosaurus*-sized prosauropod called *Ammosaurus*.

MELANOROSAURUS

RANGE OF PROSAUROPODS

During the Triassic Period, sauropods ranged all over Pangaea, the world's landmass. *Melanorosaurus* lived in South Africa, *Thecodontosaurus* in western Europe, *Anchisaurus* in western North America, and *Riojasaurus* in South America. Other prosauropods, such as *Plateosaurus* and the *Plateosaurus*-like *Lufengosaurus*, lived in what is now China. They were all extinct by Middle Jurassic times.

TRIASSIC 248-206 MYA	EARLY/MID JURASSIC 206-159 MYA	LATE JURASSIC 159-144 MYA	EARLY CRETACEOUS 144-99 MYA	LATE CRETACEOUS 99-65 MYA

SAUROPODS

STOMACH STONES

The small head and mouth of sauropods were not designed for chewing. To help break down food, they swallowed stones, which ground up plant material. We know this because gastroliths (stomach stones) have been found among their bones. Today, many plant-eating birds do the same.

The biggest dinosaurs were long-necked plant eaters known as sauropods ("lizard feet"). They had elephantine bodies, legs like tree trunks, small heads on top of long necks, and long, whiplike tails. They were related to the meat-eating dinosaurs and to the prosauropods, evolving in the Early Jurassic and dying off in Cretaceous times.

DIPLODOCUS

Perhaps the best known of the long sauropods is *Diplodocus*. At 88 feet (27 m) long, it was one of several sauropods that roamed North America in Late Jurassic times. The way the neck bones were articulated tells us they browsed on low ferny vegetation, probably sweeping out great arcs with their long necks.

SAUROPOD FRAME

Remains of sauropod skeletons consist of massive pieces of fossilized bone, so big there is nothing alive today that compares with them. In one of the latest techniques, very basic bone shapes are programmed into a computer and manipulated to let us see how the various pieces moved against one another.

TRACES OF LIFESTYLE

We used to think sauropods were too heavy to spend much time on land and must have supported their vast bulk by wading in deep water. However, we now know (mostly from fossilized footprints) that sauropods moved about in herds on dry land. Large and small footprints found together show that different sauropods lived in groups. Because there is no sign of tail marks in the tracks, they must have kept their tails raised.

SHUNOSAURUS

DIPLODOCUS

IN DEFENSE

Sauropods would have been prey to the big carnivorous dinosaurs. Just as today tigers do not attack fully grown elephants, in Jurassic times the biggest of the sauropods would have been safe from the meat eaters, but the young and the sick would have been under constant threat. *Diplodocus* probably protected itself and its herd by using its long tapering tail as a whip. *Shunosaurus*, which lived in China during the Middle Jurassic, probably used the small club on the end of its tail to defend itself.

| TRIASSIC 248-206 MYA | EARLY/MID JURASSIC 206-159 MYA | LATE JURASSIC 159-144 MYA | EARLY CRETACEOUS 144-99 MYA | LATE CRETACEOUS 99-65 MYA |

APATOSAURUS GROWTH RATE

It is difficult to tell how long a dinosaur lived. Sometimes, growth lines in the bones (like the rings of trees) suggest the animal grew more quickly at some time each year. Its age can be assessed by counting the lines. Studies of the bones of *Apatosaurus* (previously known as *Brontosaurus*), a relative of *Diplodocus*, suggest these sauropods grew quickly, without growth rings, for about 10 years. By then, they had reached 90 percent of their adult size.

10 YEARS

BRACHIOSAURUS

Although many remains have been found in the Morrison Formation, the best skeleton of *Brachiosaurus* was found halfway across the globe in Tanzania. This shows that in Late Jurassic times, Pangaea (*see pages 4-5*) had not yet split completely and the same types of dinosaur lived all over the world. A German expedition unearthed this skeleton in 1909, when Tanzania was known as German East Africa. The complete skeleton, the biggest mounted anywhere, is in the Humboldt Museum in Berlin.

TRIASSIC 248-206 MYA	EARLY/MID JURASSIC 206-159 MYA	LATE JURASSIC 159-144 MYA	EARLY CRETACEOUS 144-99 MYA	LATE CRETACEOUS 99-65 MYA

THE HEYDAY OF THE SAUROPODS

During the Late Jurassic, sauropods were at their most widespread. Some were long and low and browsed low vegetation. Others were tall and browsed lower branches of trees. There were two main types, as distinguished by the shape of their teeth. *Diplodocus* and the other long, low sauropods had peglike teeth, while the taller, stouter sauropods, such as *Brachiosaurus*, had thick, spoon-shaped teeth that indicate a different type of feeding arrangement. However, nobody is sure what it was.

DINOSAUR DETECTIVES

Often, when the remains of a very big animal are discovered, there are tantalizingly few bones found. Comparing them directly to a more complete skeleton can give us some idea of the kind of animal they came from. In 1999, four neck vertebrae of a gigantic sauropod were found. The *Sauroposeidon* bones turned out to be very similar to the neck bones of *Brachiosaurus*. So we are fairly sure *Sauroposeidon* was an animal very much like *Brachiosaurus* — but bigger!

SEISMOSAURUS

The longest dinosaur known is *Seismosaurus*. Imagine *Diplodocus*, then double its length. Make this length by stretching the neck and the tail in proportion to the body, and this is what *Seismosaurus* looked like. So far, only one *Seismosaurus* skeleton has been found, and that was in the Morrison Formation rocks in New Mexico. The skeleton is of an animal that may have been about 164 feet (50 m) long.

DRESSED TO IMPRESS

Not only did late sauropods have armor, but some had spines and frills as well. *Amargasaurus* from Early Cretaceous Argentina had a double row of spines down its neck and a tall fin down its back. Unusual sauropods evolved in Cretaceous South America because it was an island continent, and evolution took an independent direction.

ARGENTINOSAURUS

So far, the heaviest dinosaur ever found is *Argentinosaurus*. We have only six vertebrae, a part of its hips, a bit of rib, and a leg bone. The leg bone is as tall as a man. From this we believe the animal was about 88 feet (27 m) long and weighed about 55 tons. Like some earlier Morrison Formation sauropods, *Argentinosaurus* had vertebrae made of thin struts and sheets of bone with great hollows between them — a strong but light construction vital for a huge animal.

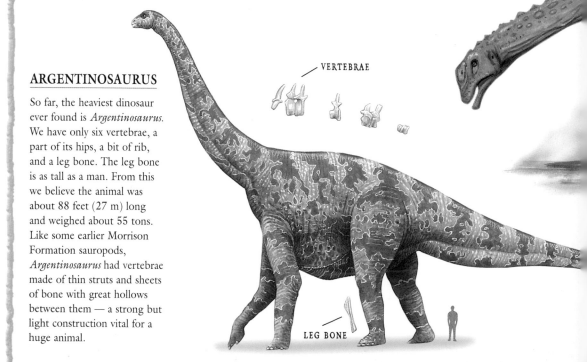

VERTEBRAE

LEG BONE

THE LAST OF THE SAUROPODS

As the world passed from the Jurassic into the Cretaceous Period, vegetation began to change and the continents moved apart. Different dinosaurs were becoming prominent. The sauropods began to die away as a completely different group of plant-eating dinosaurs evolved. In some places, the sauropods still thrived, either because the old style vegetation still flourished in some environments or because they lived on isolated continents where the new dinosaurs did not reach. Despite the spread of the new dinosaur types, there were sauropods existing to the very end of the Mesozoic Era.

TOUGH GUY

The bony armor pieces from the back of a titanosaurid were found as long ago as 1890 in Madagascar. The paleontologist who first identified them was not believed, because no other sauropod was known to be covered with armor. Only with the discovery of armored titanosaurids in Argentina in the 1970s and a more complete armored titanosaurid in Madagascar in the 1990s was this scientist's theory proven correct.

SALTASAURUS

Of the sauropods that survived into the Cretaceous Period, the titanosaurids (such as *Saltasaurus* in Argentina or *Ampelosaurus* in France) were perhaps the most successful. Despite their name, at about 39 feet (12 m) long, they were not particularly big for sauropods. In recent years, it has been found that at least some titanosaurids had a back covered with armor. This may not have been for defense; like the shell on the back of a crab, it might have been for stiffening the backbone to help the animal carry its weight.

TRIASSIC 248-206 MYA	EARLY/MID JURASSIC 206-159 MYA	LATE JURASSIC 159-144 MYA	EARLY CRETACEOUS 144-99 MYA	LATE CRETACEOUS 99-65 MYA

ORNITHOPODS - THE BIRD FEET

HYPSILOPHODON SKULL

The skull of an ornithopod was different from that of a sauropod. There was always a beak at the front for cropping food. The teeth were not merely for raking in leaves but were designed for chewing them, either by chopping or grinding. Depressions at each side of the skull show where there were probably cheek pouches used to hold the food while it was being processed. This is a far more complicated arrangement than that of the prosauropods and sauropods.

During the Triassic, at about the same time as meat eaters and prosauropods appeared, another group of plant eaters appeared. What made them different was their hipbones, which gave more space to the big intestines plant eaters needed yet enabled them to balance on their hind legs. Scientists in the 1800s called these plant eaters sauropods ("lizard feet") because they had a lizard-like arrangement of bones in their feet; the two-footed, bird-hipped dinosaurs they called ornithopods ("bird feet").

ADVANCED JAWS

Later, more advanced ornithopods had complex chewing mechanisms. An animal like *Iguanodon* (*see page 17*) or a hadrosaur (*see pages 18–19*) had its upper teeth mounted on articulated plates at each side of the skull. As the lower jaw rose, these plates moved outward to allow the sloping chewing surfaces of both sets of teeth to grind past one another. This constant milling action wore away the teeth, and new ones grew to replace them.

SAUROPOD

ORNITHOPOD

HIPBONES

As with the prosauropods (*see pages 6–7*), the hipbones of the sauropods incorporated a pubic bone that pointed down and forward. This meant the big plant-digesting intestines had to be carried forward of the hips. In ornithopods, this pubic bone is swept back, except for a pair of forward extensions that splayed out to the side. The big plant-digesting intestines could be carried beneath the animal's hipbone, closer to its center of gravity. This enabled the ornithopod to walk on its hind legs, balanced by its tail — just like a meat-eating dinosaur.

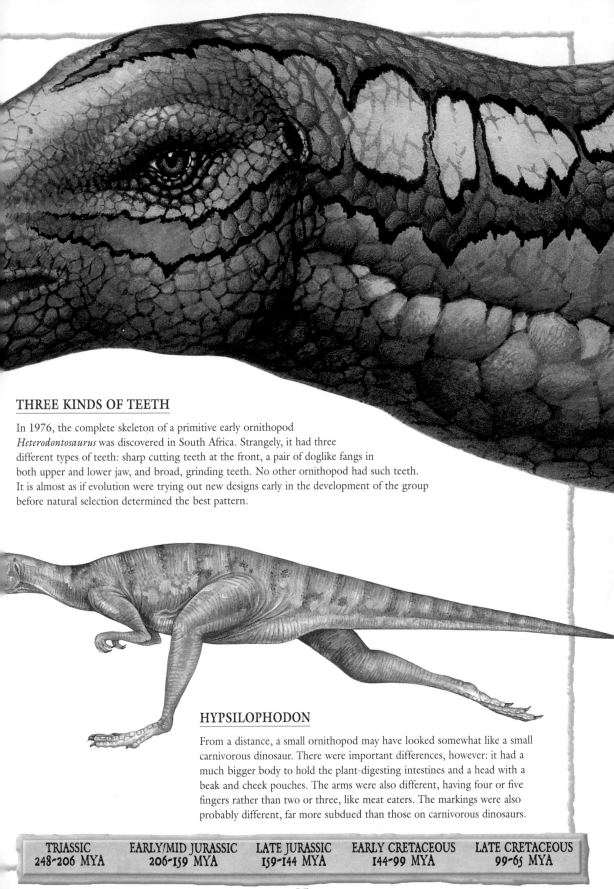

THREE KINDS OF TEETH

In 1976, the complete skeleton of a primitive early ornithopod
Heterodontosaurus was discovered in South Africa. Strangely, it had three
different types of teeth: sharp cutting teeth at the front, a pair of doglike fangs in
both upper and lower jaw, and broad, grinding teeth. No other ornithopod had such teeth.
It is almost as if evolution were trying out new designs early in the development of the group
before natural selection determined the best pattern.

HYPSILOPHODON

From a distance, a small ornithopod may have looked somewhat like a small
carnivorous dinosaur. There were important differences, however: it had a
much bigger body to hold the plant-digesting intestines and a head with a
beak and cheek pouches. The arms were also different, having four or five
fingers rather than two or three, like meat eaters. The markings were also
probably different, far more subdued than those on carnivorous dinosaurs.

TRIASSIC	EARLY/MID JURASSIC	LATE JURASSIC	EARLY CRETACEOUS	LATE CRETACEOUS
248-206 MYA	206-159 MYA	159-144 MYA	144-99 MYA	99-65 MYA

CHANGING FACE

Over the years, as more specimens were found, *Iguanodon*'s appearance changed. In the 1850s, it was constructed in the Crystal Palace gardens in London, along the lines of Mantell's big lizard. Then, in 1878, a whole herd of *Iguanodon* skeletons, mostly complete, were found in a coal mine in Bernissart, Belgium. These animals were up to 33 feet (10 m) long and had hind legs that were much longer than their forelimbs. This evidence led to reconstructions of *Iguanodon* sitting on its hind legs, resting on its tail like a kangaroo — an image that was accepted for the next century.

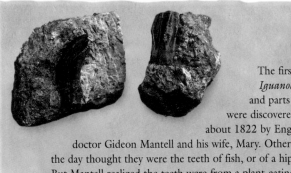

IGUANA TOOTH

The first remains of *Iguanodon* — teeth and parts of bones — were discovered in Kent in about 1822 by English country doctor Gideon Mantell and his wife, Mary. Other scientists of the day thought they were the teeth of fish, or of a hippopotamus. But Mantell realized the teeth were from a plant-eating reptile like a modern iguana lizard. His first reconstructions showed a kind of a dragon-sized, iguana-like reptile, similar to the first reconstructions of the meat-eating *Megalosaurus*, also recently discovered.

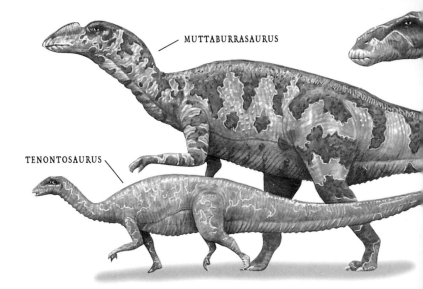

MUTTABURRASAURUS

TENONTOSAURUS

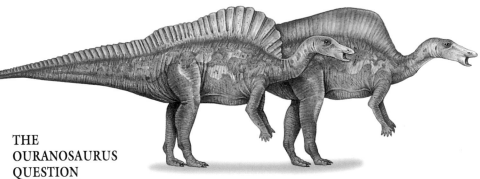

THE OURANOSAURUS QUESTION

One iguanodontid, *Ouranosaurus*, had an arrangement of tall spines forming a kind of picket fence along its backbone, probably to support some sort of fin or sail. Since *Ouranosaurus* lived in North Africa, which was hot and arid during Cretaceous times, such a sail could have regulated its body temperature by exposing blood vessels to the warming sun and cooling wind. A meat eater, *Spinosaurus*, lived in the same time and place and also had a sail. Another theory is that the spines supported a fatty hump, such as camels have today.

THE IGUANODON DYNASTY

Iguanodon was among the first dinosaurs to be discovered. The teeth and a few scraps of bone were found first and were obviously from a large plant-eating reptile. At the time, few people were familiar with modern plant-eating reptiles, so the animal was particularly unusual. Some scientific work was being done on the modern South American plant-eating lizard, the iguana, which had teeth somewhat like those of this new fossil. Hence, it was given the name *Iguanodon*.

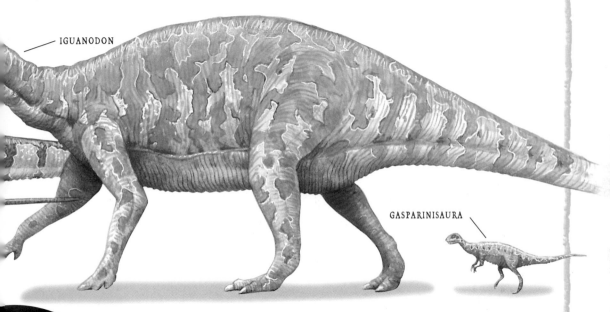

IGUANODON

GASPARINISAURA

MEET THE FAMILY

The modern view of *Iguanodon* is that it was too heavy to spend much time on its hind legs, so it moved on all fours. Since it was discovered, scientists have found many more iguanodontids. Australian *Muttaburrasaurus* was slightly smaller. American *Tenontosaurus* had a particularly long tail. The most primitive member of the group was *Gasparinisaura* from Argentina, the size of a turkey.

IGUANODON FOOD

Iguanodon lived in northern Europe during Early Cretaceous times. It wandered in herds across swampy landscapes, knee-deep in reed-beds of horsetail plants that grew just like our modern species. The herds probably grazed on these horsetails as they moved from one area to another.

TRIASSIC	EARLY/MID JURASSIC	LATE JURASSIC	EARLY CRETACEOUS	LATE CRETACEOUS
248-206 MYA	206-159 MYA	159-144 MYA	144-99 MYA	99-65 MYA

THE DUCKBILLS

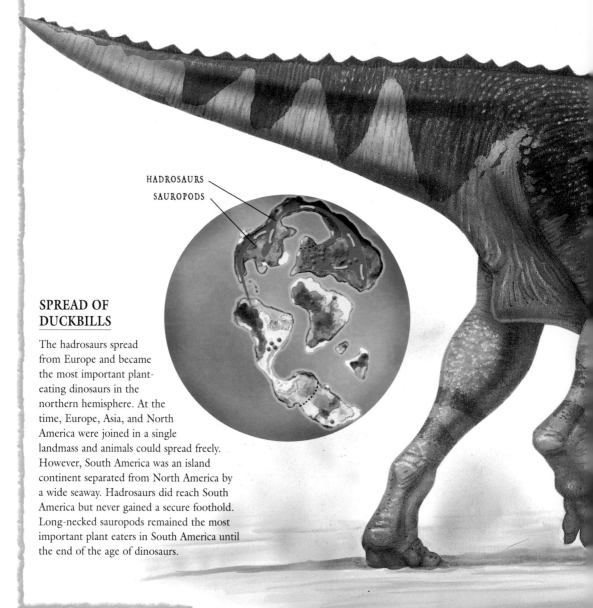

In the Late Cretaceous, a new group of ornithopods evolved from the iguanodontids. The vegetation was changing: primitive forests were giving way to modern-looking woodlands of oak, beech, and other broad-leaved trees with undergrowth of flowering herbs. These new dinosaurs, the hadrosaurs, spread and flourished in the forests throughout Europe, Asia, and North America. They had thousands of grinding teeth and a broad beak at the front of the mouth.

HADROSAURS
SAUROPODS

SPREAD OF DUCKBILLS

The hadrosaurs spread from Europe and became the most important plant-eating dinosaurs in the northern hemisphere. At the time, Europe, Asia, and North America were joined in a single landmass and animals could spread freely. However, South America was an island continent separated from North America by a wide seaway. Hadrosaurs did reach South America but never gained a secure foothold. Long-necked sauropods remained the most important plant eaters in South America until the end of the age of dinosaurs.

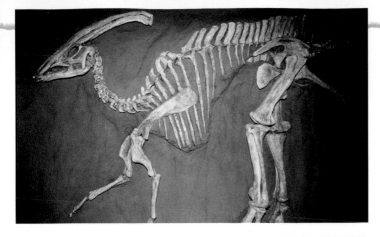

HEAD CRESTS

Some hadrosaurs, like this *Parasaurolophus*, had elaborate head crests. Mostly made of hollow bone connected to the nostrils, they were probably used for signaling one another through dense forests. Each type of hadrosaur had a unique crest shape to distinguish different herds from one another. Those with flat heads or solid crests probably supported an inflatable flap of skin that could have been puffed up like a frog's throat to make a noise.

MODERN CONIFERS

Modern conifers, such as pine and spruce, as well as the broad-leaved trees, such as oak and ash, appeared in Cretaceous times. Until then, the more primitive conifers, such as monkey puzzle trees, had sustained the sauropods. Hadrosaurs were well equipped for dealing with the new conifers. They used their broad beaks to scrape off the needles and their batteries of teeth to grind them down before swallowing.

HADROSAURUS

Hadrosaurus was, like *Iguanodon*, essentially a two-footed, plant-eating dinosaur which as an adult would have been rather too heavy to spend much time on its hind legs. It would have moved about on all fours, a theory confirmed by the fleshy, weight-bearing pads on its forelimbs. *Hadrosaurus'* tail was very deep and flat, which once led scientists to think the hadrosaur may have been a swimming animal — an idea that has now been discarded. Its most distinctive feature was its broad, flat, duck-like beak.

TRIASSIC 248-206 MYA	EARLY/MID JURASSIC 206-159 MYA	LATE JURASSIC 159-144 MYA	EARLY CRETACEOUS 144-99 MYA	LATE CRETACEOUS 99-65 MYA

DEATH OF DENVER STEGOSAURUS

A team from the Denver Museum discovered a *Stegosaurus* skeleton with a diseased tail after a broken tail spike became infected. The weakened animal then died during a drought. Its stomach bloated, rolling it over on its back. The drought ended and a nearby river burst its banks, covering the *Stegosaurus* with silt. All this was deduced 140 million years later from the fossil and the types of rocks found nearby. Such study of what leads to fossilization is known as *taphonomy*.

STEGOSAURUS

Stegosaurus lived in North America at the end of the Jurassic Period. A big four-footed animal up to 26 feet (8 m) long, with shorter legs at the front, a double row of plates along its back, and two pairs of spikes sticking out toward the tip of its tail, it had a small head and a kind of armored mesh protecting its throat. Some scientists believe the plates formed an armored shield. Others insist they acted as heat exchangers to cool its blood by turning the plates to the wind or to absorb warmth from the Sun.

SMALL BRAIN

The head of a Ste*gosaurus* was quite small and held a very small brain. Like ornithopods, it had a beak at the front of its mouth and cheeks along the side.

| TRIASSIC 248-206 MYA | EARLY/MID JURASSIC 206-159 MYA | LATE JURASSIC 159-144 MYA | EARLY CRETACEOUS 144-99 MYA | LATE CRETACEOUS 99-65 MYA |

THE PLATED LIZARDS

Not long after ornithopods came into existence, all kinds of other dinosaurs began to evolve from them. Many sported armor of one kind or another. They were too heavy to spend much time on two legs and became mostly four-footed beasts. One group had armor arranged in a double row of plates or spikes down its back and tail. These plated dinosaurs were known as stegosaurs.

FLAT

PAIRS

SINGLE OVERLAPPING ROW

DOUBLE ALTERNATING

UNDER ATTACK

PLATE PUZZLES

The back plates of *Stegosaurus* were embedded in its skin but not attached directly to its skeleton. This has caused uncertainty about how they were arranged. One theory suggests that the plates lay flat as armor along the animal's back. Another is that they stood upright in pairs. Yet another says they had a single upright row of overlapping plates. The most widely accepted view is that they stood in a double row, alternating with one another. Some scientists suggest that the muscles at the base of the plates would have allowed *Stegosaurus* to point them at an attacker.

A WORLD OF STEGOSAURS

CLEVER TAIL

Most stegosaurids had two pairs of spikes at the end of their tail. The tails were usually quite flexible and could have been swung sideways with some force against the flanks of an attacker. In the hipbones was a gap that may have held a concentration of nerves to control the hind legs and tail and a gland that supplied extra energy. This space in the tail gave rise to a once-popular misconception that stegosaurids had two brains.

Stegosaurus was not the only stegosaurid. There were many others, ranging from North America through Europe to Asia. They probably evolved from an Early Jurassic group called the scelidosaurids. The most primitive of the stegosaurids we know were found in Middle Jurassic rocks in China. From such medium-sized animals developed a wide range of plated and spiked dinosaurs. By the Middle Cretaceous they had all but died out. The remains of a possible stegosaurid were found in Upper Cretaceous rocks in India. Perhaps the group lasted longer in India, an island continent at the time.

KENTROSAURUS ————

EAST AFRICAN DISCOVERIES

The Humboldt Museum in Berlin has a collection of Late Jurassic dinosaurs excavated from East Africa in the 1920s. Among them are the stegosaurid *Kentrosaurus*, which was very similar to the North American *Stegosaurus*. There were also sauropods such as *Dicraeosaurus* (shown left), which was similar to *Diplodocus*.

AN EARLY STEGOSAURID

Cow-sized *Scelidosaurus*, known from the Lower Jurassic rocks of England, was a four-footed herbivore covered with small studs of armor. It may have been an ancestor of the stegosaurids or of the later Cretaceous nodosaurids of North America and the Middle Jurassic to Late Cretaceous ankylosaurids of Europe, North America, and Asia. It may even have been ancestral to both.

VARIETY OF STEGOSAURIDS

The most primitive stegosaurid known is the 13-foot- (4-m-) long *Huayangosaurus* from Middle Jurassic China. Later stegosaurids had shorter front legs, but the legs of *Huayangosaurus* hardly varied. Its armor included paired narrow back spikes and a tail with two pairs of spikes. It also had a pair of shoulder spikes, as did some later stegosaurids. *Dacenturus* (Late Jurassic Europe) had low, rounded plates on its shoulders and back and tall spikes down its tail. *Kentrosaurus* (Late Jurassic Africa) had its center of gravity at its hips, so, like some sauropods, it could rise on its hind legs to browse (as could *Stegosaurus*). *Wuerhosaurus* (Early Cretaceous China) was as big as *Stegosaurus* and had long low back plates.

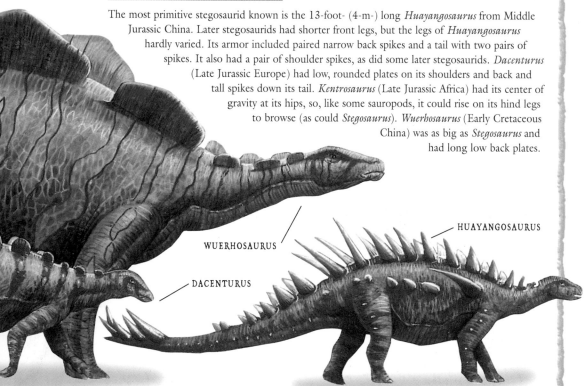

WUERHOSAURUS

DACENTURUS

HUAYANGOSAURUS

TRIASSIC 248-206 MYA	EARLY/MID JURASSIC 206-159 MYA	LATE JURASSIC 159-144 MYA	EARLY CRETACEOUS 144-99 MYA	LATE CRETACEOUS 99-65 MYA

THE NODOSAURIDS - SPIKY DINOSAURS

As the Jurassic Period passed, the armored stegosaurids became extinct and other groups of armored dinosaurs evolved. The two most closely related groups were the nodosaurids and the ankylosaurids. Each had small, bony plates across their broad backs. These plates stretched up the neck to the head and down the tail and would have had horny covers that made the animal's back impregnable. The distinctive feature of the nodosaurid group was the presence of long, tough spikes sticking out sideways and upward from the shoulders and from the sides.

GASTONIA

One of the best-preserved nodosaurid fossils ever found was *Gastonia*. Its armor formed a solid shield. Spikes stood up over the shoulders, and it had a series of broad, flat spines, almost blades, sticking outward and running down each side from the neck to the tip of the tail. It was found in Early Cretaceous rocks in Utah, but an almost identical Early Cretaceous dinosaur has been found in England.

SPIKY CUSTOMERS

Two related groups of armored dinosaurs existed in Cretaceous times. The nodosaurids were characterized by spikes on the neck and sides, while the ankylosaurids had clubs on the ends of their tails.

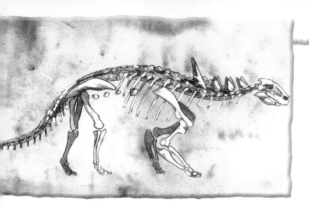

SAUROPELTA SKELETON

The solid back plate armor is the most commonly fossilized part of a nodosaurid and is usually found upside down. If a nodosaurid died and fell into a river, it may have been washed out to sea. As it decayed, expanding digestive gases in its gut would have turned it over, its heavy back acting as a keel. As it settled on the seabed, it would be buried and eventually fossilized in that position.

STRUTHIOSAURUS

Not all nodosaurids were big animals. *Struthiosaurus* from Upper Cretaceous rocks of central Europe was only 6.5 feet (2 m) long, with a body the size of a dog. It was probably an island dweller. Island animals, such as the modern Shetland pony, tend to evolve into smaller forms to make best use of limited food.

SAUROPELTA

One of the earliest nodosaurids was *Sauropelta* of Montana and Wyoming. It had an arched back, long tail, and longer hind legs. Like all other nodosaurids, its neck, back, and tail were covered with armor. *Sauropelta*'s long, defensive spines were confined to the neck and shoulders and spread outward and upward.

TRIASSIC 248-206 MYA	EARLY/MID JURASSIC 206-159 MYA	LATE JURASSIC 159-144 MYA	EARLY CRETACEOUS 144-99 MYA	LATE CRETACEOUS 99-65 MYA

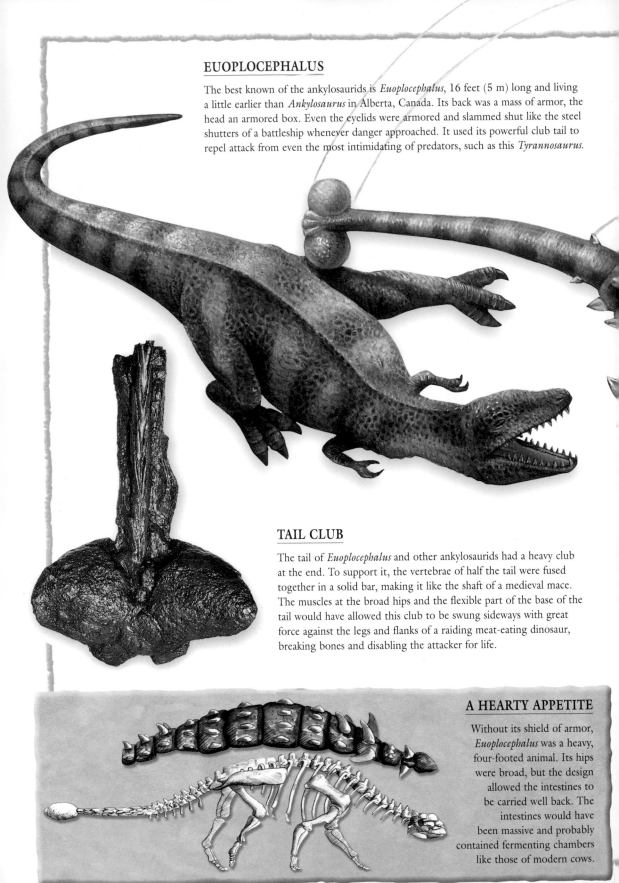

EUOPLOCEPHALUS

The best known of the ankylosaurids is *Euoplocephalus*, 16 feet (5 m) long and living a little earlier than *Ankylosaurus* in Alberta, Canada. Its back was a mass of armor, the head an armored box. Even the eyelids were armored and slammed shut like the steel shutters of a battleship whenever danger approached. It used its powerful club tail to repel attack from even the most intimidating of predators, such as this *Tyrannosaurus*.

TAIL CLUB

The tail of *Euoplocephalus* and other ankylosaurids had a heavy club at the end. To support it, the vertebrae of half the tail were fused together in a solid bar, making it like the shaft of a medieval mace. The muscles at the broad hips and the flexible part of the base of the tail would have allowed this club to be swung sideways with great force against the legs and flanks of a raiding meat-eating dinosaur, breaking bones and disabling the attacker for life.

A HEARTY APPETITE

Without its shield of armor, *Euoplocephalus* was a heavy, four-footed animal. Its hips were broad, but the design allowed the intestines to be carried well back. The intestines would have been massive and probably contained fermenting chambers like those of modern cows.

ANKYLOSAURIDS - THE CLUB-TAILS

Ankylosaurids were closely related to nodosaurids but mostly came later, toward the end of the Cretaceous. With their armored necks and backs, they looked like their relatives, but instead of having spikes on the shoulders and sides, they had a heavy, bony club at the end of the tail. This could have been devastating when swung at an enemy. It may also have been used as a decoy. Perhaps it looked like a head on a neck, causing meat eaters to attack it instead of the more vulnerable front end.

CRETACEOUS UNDERGROWTH

By the end of the Cretaceous Period, modern plants had evolved. Beneath the broad-leaved trees was an undergrowth of flowering herbs such as buttercups. The ankylosaurids and the nodosaurids carried their heads low and their mouths close to the ground. They were evidently low-level feeders that ate the flowering herbs.

TRIASSIC 248-206 MYA	EARLY/MID JURASSIC 206-159 MYA	LATE JURASSIC 159-144 MYA	EARLY CRETACEOUS 144-99 MYA	LATE CRETACEOUS 99-65 MYA

HEADS

Each group of pachycephalosaurids had its own type of skull shape and ornamentation. *Stegoceras* and *Homalocephale*, from Mongolia, had sloping heads, higher at the rear, the latter with an elaborate head crest. *Prenocephale*, also from Mongolia, had a more rounded, dome-like head. Both had decorative lumps around the bony crown. North American *Stygimoloch* was perhaps the strangest, with a weird array of spikes and spines all around its dome. These were probably used for intimidation rather than fighting. All pachycephalosaurids lived in the Late Cretaceous Period.

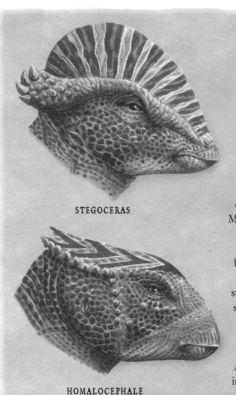

STEGOCERAS

HOMALOCEPHALE

STYGIMOLOCH

PRENOCEPHALE

MODERN SPARRERS

In the North American Rocky Mountains, modern bighorn sheep and mountain goats go through an annual ritual in which the males fight the flock leader to test his strength. The construction of their skulls and horns protects them from suffering much damage when they bash against one another. Pachycephalosaurids probably had similar rituals.

TRIASSIC 248-206 MYA	EARLY/MID JURASSIC 206-159 MYA	LATE JURASSIC 159-144 MYA	EARLY CRETACEOUS 144-99 MYA	LATE CRETACEOUS 99-65 MYA

BONEHEADS

Imagine a dinosaur, a two-footed, plant-eating dinosaur such as an ornithopod, but give it a very high forehead so it looks brainy. What you would have is a pachycephalosaurid — another dinosaur group descended from the ornithopods. The intelligent look is actually false. The brain in that head is tiny, and the roof of the skull is made up of thick bone. We think the bone on top of the head was a weapon — a kind of battering ram. This was probably not for use against predators but for display in courtship battles.

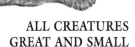

ALL CREATURES GREAT AND SMALL

There was a great range of sizes in pachycephalosaurids. The largest known, at 16 feet (5 m) long, was North American *Pachycephalosaurus*. The smallest was *Micropachycephalosaurus* from China, which was about the size of a rabbit. This very small dinosaur has the longest dinosaur name ever given.

HORNED BATTLERS

Stegoceras is the most complete known pachycephalosaurid. Its head bone and strong neck provided great protection. They seem to have lived in herds. The males probably fought each other to lead the herd; the strongest would mate with the females.

HARD HEADS

Dinosaur skulls are rarely preserved as fossils, but pachycephalosaurid skulls were different. The top bone of the skull was so massive it often survived as a fossil. Commonly the only part of the animal preserved, these skulls are often found very battered. This suggests they were washed down a river for long distances before being buried in sediment. This may mean that these were mountain-living animals.

THE PRIMITIVE-HORNED DINOSAURS

The last of the plant-eating dinosaur groups existed from the mid to Late Cretaceous. Like the ankylosaurids and the nodosaurids, they lived in North America and in Asia, and they also evolved from ornithopods. They were equipped with armor, but it was confined solely to the head. Early types were lightly built and very ornithopod-like, but in later forms the armor on the head became so heavy that they moved around as four-footed animals. Flamboyant neck shields and horns evolved, and these horned dinosaurs became known as the ceratopsians.

AN EARLY SHEEP

Scientists regard *Protoceratops* as the sheep of Late Cretaceous Mongolia. Similar in size to sheep, they lived in herds and grazed the sparse vegetation of the arid landscape. One particular skeleton was found with the skeleton of a fierce carnivore, *Velociraptor*, clinging to its head shield. The meat eater had attacked the ceratopsian with its killing claws, but the ceratopsian must have fought back with its big beak; both dinosaurs lost their lives during the fight.

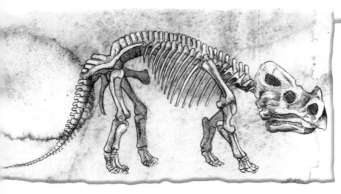

BIG BROTHER

By the time *Montanoceratops* had evolved, toward the end of the Late Cretaceous, ceratopsians were bigger and had developed horns. *Montanoceratops* was about 10 feet (3 m) long and walked on all fours. Like its two-footed ancestors, however, it had claws on its feet. In later ceratopsians, the toenails developed into hooves, which were better able to carry the weight of big animals.

ARCHAEOCERATOPS

The most primitive of the ceratopsians known is *Archaeoceratops*. It was a very small animal, about 3 feet (1 m) long, and scampered nimbly on hind legs on the plains of Early Cretaceous China. It had a head that was very similar to that of *Psittacosaurus*. Its skeleton was so primitive and generalized it is possible that its descendants gave rise to the big ceratopsians that were to follow.

WHO'S A PRETTY BOY?

An early relative of the ceratopsians was the 5-foot- (1.5-m-) long parrot-lizard *Psittacosaurus*. It developed a very strong beak and powerful jaws for plucking and chopping the tough vegetation it ate. A bony ridge around the back of the skull anchored its strong jaw muscles. The bony ridge and its big beak gave the skull a square shape, and the head must have looked a bit like the big-beaked head of a modern parrot.

CYCAD FOSSIL

At the end of the Cretaceous Period, the old-style vegetation was largely replaced by modern species of plants. However, some of the older types of palmlike cycads remained in some regions. In the areas where they occurred, the ceratopsians may have relied on these plants. Their narrow beaks could have reached into the palmlike clump of fronds and selected the best pieces, and their strong jaws could have shredded the tough leaves.

TRIASSIC 248-206 MYA	EARLY/MID JURASSIC 206-159 MYA	LATE JURASSIC 159-144 MYA	EARLY CRETACEOUS 144-99 MYA	LATE CRETACEOUS 99-65 MYA

VARIETY OF HEADS

CHASMOSAURUS

STYRACOSAURUS

Ceratopsians all had the same body shape, but their different shapes of shield and horn arrangements made each type easily recognizable to its own herd. *Styracosaurus* had a monumental horn on its nose and an array of horns around its shield. *Chasmosaurus* had an enormous, sail-like shield. *Einiosaurus* had a long nose horn that curved forward and a pair of straight horns at the edge of its shield. *Acheluosaurus* had a battering ram on its nose, a pair of short, bladelike horns above its eyes, and a curved pair at the shield-edge.

ALL FOR ONE

The horns of ceratopsians would have been used to defend themselves and their herd against big carnivores and also to tussle with one another over position in the herd. Having locked horns, they would have pushed and shoved until one of them gave way. Little harm would have come to the loser. While traveling, the ceratopsians may have kept their young at the center of the herd to protect them. If attacked by carnivores, they may have formed a circle with the youngsters in the center and the adults facing outward so that the attackers were faced with the shields and horns of all the herd. Today, musk oxen protect their herd this way.

WILDEBEEST

We know ceratopsians moved in herds because we have found bone beds consisting of many hundreds, even thousands, of skeletons. The animals would have been migrating, traveling in herds to areas where there was more food at a particular time of year. When crossing a river, they may have been caught by a sudden flash flood that washed them away and dumped their bodies. This still happens in Africa today as herds of wildebeest migrate from one feeding ground to another.

THE BIG-HORNED DINOSAURS

EINIOSAURUS

CHELUOSAURUS

The big ceratopsians were probably the most spectacular Late Cretaceous dinosaurs. They were all four-footed and mostly as big as today's rhinoceros. The ridge of bone around the neck had evolved into a broad shield. They also had an array of long horns on the face. The skulls of the big ceratopsians were so tough that many were preserved as fossils. There were two main lines of evolution. One group developed long frills and a pair of long horns above the eyes; the other had shorter frills and tended to have a single horn on the nose.

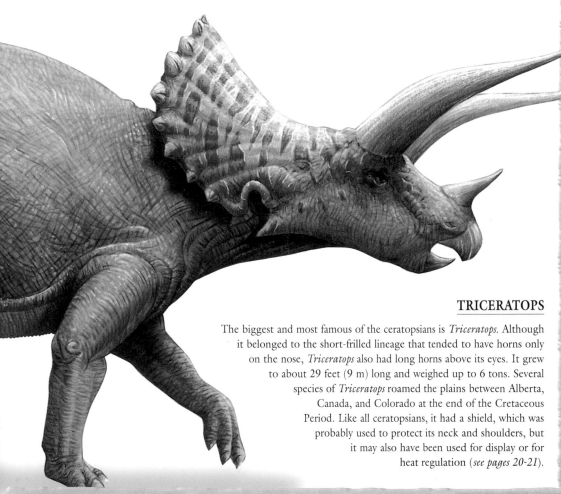

TRICERATOPS

The biggest and most famous of the ceratopsians is *Triceratops.* Although it belonged to the short-frilled lineage that tended to have horns only on the nose, *Triceratops* also had long horns above its eyes. It grew to about 29 feet (9 m) long and weighed up to 6 tons. Several species of *Triceratops* roamed the plains between Alberta, Canada, and Colorado at the end of the Cretaceous Period. Like all ceratopsians, it had a shield, which was probably used to protect its neck and shoulders, but it may also have been used for display or for heat regulation (*see pages 20-21*).

TRIASSIC 248-206 MYA	EARLY/MID JURASSIC 206-159 MYA	LATE JURASSIC 159-144 MYA	EARLY CRETACEOUS 144-99 MYA	LATE CRETACEOUS 99-65 MYA

DID YOU KNOW?

• Dinosaurs are given long, scientific names that are usually based on Latin or ancient Greek words. Scientists all over the world can then understand the names, no matter what language they usually speak.

• Scientific names for dinosaurs have two parts, like *Tyrannosaurus rex.* The first part of any plant or animal's scientific name is its genus name, and the second part is the species name. Usually, when the name is not used in a scientific setting, only the genus name is used. However, the full name is sometimes so impressive that people use it all the time. If we did this, however, we would refer to *Triceratops* as *Triceratops prorsus.* When writing, scientists use an animal's full scientific name the first time, but they shorten it after that by replacing the genus part with its initial. For example, *Tyrannosaurus rex* becomes *T. rex.* Scientific names are always printed in italics. The genus part always has a capital letter, but the species part does not. These rules hold even if the name is based on the name of a person or a place — for example, *Protoceratops andrewsii.*

• Dinosaur names sometimes change. Old books usually call *Apatosaurus* "*Brontosaurus.*" Arthur Lakes, a collector, found the first specimen in 1877 and sent it to paleontologist Othneil Charles Marsh, who named it *Apatosaurus ajax.* Two years later, William Reed, a collector, also sent a skeleton to Marsh. *Brontosaurus excelsus* was the name Marsh gave it. Until 1974, scientists used the name *Brontosaurus.* But someone realized that both skeletons were the same dinosaur. In such cases, the first name given is the only valid one, so in 1974, *Brontosaurus* had to be dropped in favor of *Apatosaurus.*

• Sometimes scientists give a dinosaur a name that is already in use. When the bird/dinosaur *Rahonavis ostromi* was first studied in 1998, it was called *Rahona ostromi.* That was changed after someone noticed that a beetle was already named Rahona. *Mononychus* was changed to *Mononykus* for the same reason. Sometimes a change of spelling is all that is needed.

MORE BOOKS TO READ

Dinosaurs. Reader's Digest Pathfinders (series). Paul M. A. Willis (Reader's Digest)

Duckbills and Boneheads. Awesome Dinosaurs (series). Michael Benton (Copper Beech Books)

Giant Plant Eaters. Awesome Dinosaurs (series). Michael Benton (Copper Beech Books)

Stegosaurus and Other Jurassic Plant-Eaters. Daniel Cohen (Children's Press)

WEB SITES

Fossil Zone: The Place to Dig. *www.discovery.com/exp/fossilzone/ fossilzone.html*

The Gentle Giant Vegetarians. *www.facethemusic.org/fantasy/ dinoveg.html*

GLOSSARY

articulates: comes together at a certain angle at a joint.

browsed: ate or grazed upon.

conifer: a tree, such as a pine or fir, that has cones.

crests: decorative parts that stand up on the head of a bird or other animal.

cycads: tough, palmlike plants eaten by early herbivores.

drought: a long, dry period of low rainfall.

evolved: changed and developed over long periods of time so that descendants look or behave differently than their early ancestors.

expedition: a journey with a specific goal.

extinct: no longer existing or living.

fern: a plant that has feathery fronds and reproduces by spores.

flamboyant: very showy or decorated.

food chain: a feeding cycle in which each plant or animal becomes food for another, and so on.

fossilization: to become a fossil — a part or impression of an organism from a past geologic age, embedded in natural materials, such as rock or resin.

frills: ruffled or pleated borders that extend out, such as a ridge of bone.

fused: joined as if melted together.

gastroliths: stones that an animal swallows to help its digestion by grinding food.

genus: a grouping of related plants or animals. A family is the most broad grouping, a genus is next, and a species is the most specific grouping.

gut: the digestive system, including the stomach and all the intestines.

impregnable: unconquerable, cannot be gotten into.

mace: a heavy war club with a spiked head, from the Middle Ages.

migrate: to move to another land area because of a season or climate change.

natural selection: a theory that only the plants or animals that have the best characteristics to survive in a certain environment will live and reproduce.

paleontologist: a scientist who studies fossils to learn about past ages.

Pangaea: the single mass of land that existed on Earth in prehistoric times, before the continents drifted apart.

plates: smooth, flat, relatively thin bonelike structures, usually growing on the back, that helped protect herbivores.

primitive: an earlier, less complex version.

prolific: having many offspring, numerous.

ranged: could be found in certain areas.

reptiles: cold-blooded vertebrates, such as snakes, turtles, or crocodiles, that lay eggs and have horny plates or scales on their bodies.

seabed: the floor of a body of water, usually a part of an ocean.

serrated: having a toothed, notched cutting edge.

silt: mud and other fine materials that settle at the bottom of water.

species: a group of plants or animals that are very alike. A species is the most narrow, specific scientific grouping.

taphonomy: the study of how fossils of plants and animals are made.

vertebrae: the individual bones that form the spinal column, or backbone.

INDEX

ACKNOWLEDGEMENTS

The original publisher would like to thank Advocate, Helen Wire, and Elizabeth Wiggans for their assistance.

Picture Credits: t=top, b=bottom, c=center, l=left, r=right
Lisa Alderson: 11br, 14b, 15b, 16b, 24-25c, 28-29c. John Alston: 4tl, 4tr, 4b, 9cr, 10t, 18b, 20t, 21c, 27t, 31t, 32t. Australian Museum: 8tl. A-Z Botanical: 17bl, 19tr, 27cr. BBC Natural History Unit: 28b, 32b. Dr. Jose Bonaparte: 5t. Fossil Finds: 7t, 13t, 30cl, 31b.Humboldt Museum: 10cl. National Trust: 9cl. Simon Mendez: 4-5c, 6t, 6-7c, 8-9c, 10-11b, 12b, 16-17c, 20-21c, 22-23c, 26-27c, 28t, 32-33c. OFC. Museum of Utah: 26tl. Natural History Museum: 14t, 14cl, 15t, 16ct, 19t, 20b, 23cr, 24cl, 24b, 26b, 27cr, 29b, 29tr, 31cr. Luis Rey: 12t, 13c, 18-19c, 30-31c, 28cl. Professor Kent Stephens: 9t.

Every effort has been made to trace the copyright holders, and we apologize in advance for any unintentional errors or omissions.